Cars

Ruth Thomson

Watts Books
London • New York • Sydney

Note for parents and teachers

The Changing Times series is soundly based on the requirements of the new History Curriculum. Using the device of four generations of a real family, the author combines reminiscences of this family with other people's oral evidence. The oral history is matched with photographs and other contemporary sources. Many other lessons are hidden in the text, which practises the skills of chronological sequencing, gives reference to a timeline and introduces the language and vocabulary of the past. Young children will find much useful information here, as well as a new understanding of the recent history of every day situations and familiar things.

© Watts Books 1992

Paperback edition 1995

Watts Books
96 Leonard Street
London
EC2A 4RH

Franklin Watts Australia
14 Mars Road
Lane Cove
NSW 2066

UK ISBN: 0 7496 0893 5 (hardback)
UK ISBN: 0 7496 1800 0 (paperback)

Dewey Decimal Classification Number 388.3

A CIP catalogue record for this book is available from the British Library.

Editor: Sarah Ridley
Designer: Michael Leaman
Educational Consultant: John West
Photographer: Peter Millard

Acknowledgements: The publishers would like to thank the following people and organisations for their help with the preparation of this book: Nicholas, Jessie and Suzanne Ridley, Jessie Baker, Joan Blyth, Chris Gill of the National Motor Museum at Beaulieu and Nic Portway.

Printed in Malaysia

Contents

My name is Tom.
I was born in 1987.
I have got one brother
who is younger than me.

My name is Suzanne.
I am Tom's mother.
I was born in 1966.
I have got three sisters.

My name is Nick.
I am Suzanne's father
and Tom's grandfather.
I was born in 1937.

My name is Jessie.
I am Nick's mother-in-law,
Suzanne's grandmother
and Tom's great-grandmother.
I was born in 1908.

2000   1975   1950

This is our family car.
We go everywhere in it —
to school, to friends
and to Granny's.

Sometimes we go to town.
We park in a big car park.

Once a week Mum drives to the superstore to do the shopping.

When the car needs filling up,
we go to the garage.
Mum's car uses lead-free petrol.

I asked Mum what kind of car her family had when she was young.

She said,

'We had a Morris Traveller. I helped to wash it at weekends.'

Tax disc

'My Dad took me to school by car,
but most of my friends went by bus.
We also used the car for outings.'

'My Auntie Susie had a red Mini.
Minis were small and cheap.
Riding in one was a big treat.'

Mum said,

'Lots of people we knew got new cars.
Dad chatted with the neighbours
about all the different sorts.
He loved driving.'

Hillman Minx

Vauxhall Cresta

Rover 3500

Ford Consul Saloon

Citröen 2CV

Triumph Herald 1200

These are some of the cars
people owned when Mum was a child.

Ford Zephyr

Mum said,

'There was a lot of fuss when parking meters were put up in town. Nobody wanted to pay for parking. People were horrid to the traffic wardens.'

'A new shopping area was built. It was for pedestrians only.'

'When I was seven
we went up the motorway
to visit my aunt and uncle.
It felt like driving on a racetrack.
I'd never been so fast.'

'We had to pass
Spaghetti Junction.
It was a maze of roads
going over and under
each other.'

I asked Grandad whether his family had a car when he was young.

He said,

'There was a lot of excitement, when we bought our first car. It was a Ford.'

'My father didn't drive it every day, because he walked to work. We used the car to visit friends at weekends and for going on holiday.'

Grandad aged seven in 1944

1925   1900

'My father learnt to drive
before there were driving tests.
A friend taught him to drive
and then he just paid for
a driving licence.'

Milk cart

'We never used the car
to go shopping.
Delivery vans
or horse-drawn carts
came round with bread,
milk and groceries.
We grew vegetables
in the garden.'

Baker's van

13

Grandad said,

'Most people didn't have cars.
In towns, they travelled
by tram, trolleybus or bicycle.
A lot of people walked everywhere.'

'People went on day trips by
coach, charabanc or train.'

'Lots of new roads were built.'

'A garage opened quite near our house.'

'It sold several brands of petrol.'

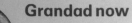

Grandad said,

'There were very few traffic lights or roundabouts. Policemen controlled the traffic at cross roads.'

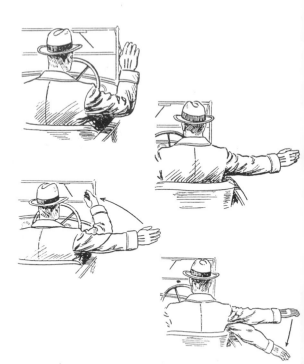

'My father's car had indicators which swung up. They were always getting stuck down, so usually he did hand signals too.'

'As the roads got busier,
people worried more about road safety.
We had lessons about it at school.'

'My dad gave me some Safety First
cigarette cards.'

When I asked Grandad
about life in wartime he said,

'During the war against Germany,
people couldn't use their cars much.
It was hard to get petrol,
because it was rationed.
We walked or cycled instead.'

Go by
SHANKS' PONY

Walk short distances

AND LEAVE ROOM FOR THOSE
WHO HAVE LONGER JOURNEYS

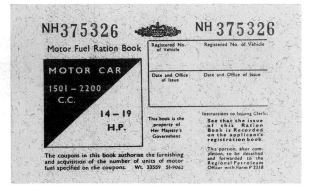

Petrol ration book

'Lights were
blacked out
after dark, so
enemy planes
couldn't see
where to bomb.
Car headlights
had to be
covered so only
a thin beam
showed.'

'Signposts were taken down, in case the Germans invaded. You really had to know your way around.'

I asked Great-granny if many people had cars
when she was young.

She said,

'When I was little,
cars were few and far between.
Horses pulled carriages and carts.'

'I walked two miles to school.
Sometimes we went by tram
to the town centre.'

Great-granny said,

'You were really somebody if you had a car.
We didn't have one, but my Auntie Maggie did.
Sometimes she took us for outings.'

'We were always having punctures because the roads were so stony.'

'There were hardly any signposts. We took maps for long journeys.'

MOTORING and HIKING Map

SECTION FF

Including—
Bridgnorth, Great Malvern, Hereford, Kidderminster, Market Drayton, Montgomery, Oswestry, Presteigne, Shrewsbury, Stoke-upon-Trent, Wellington, Whitchurch, Worcester

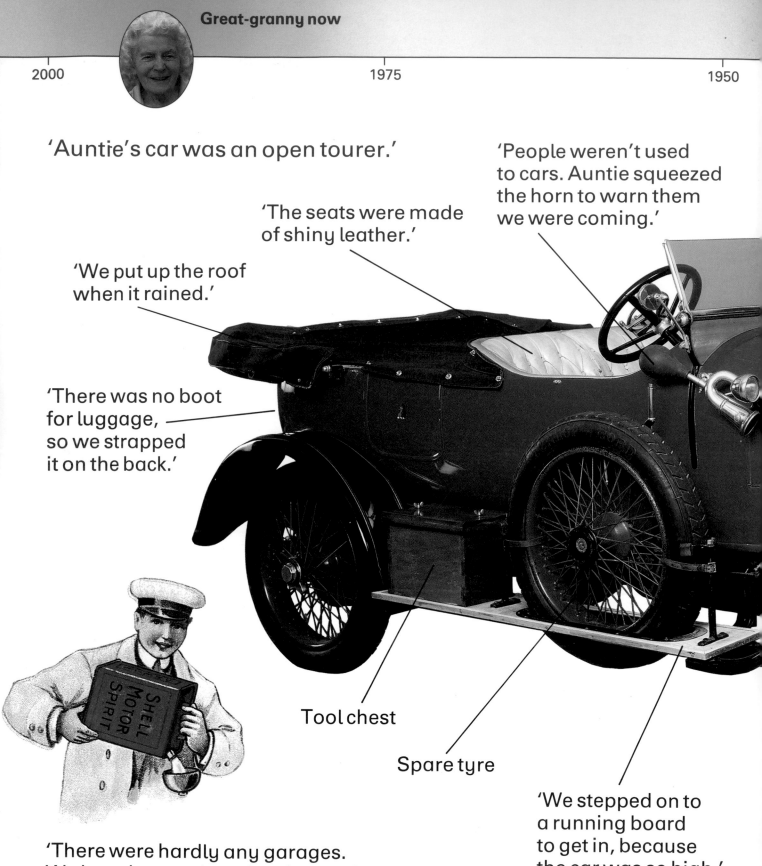

'Auntie's car was an open tourer.'

'People weren't used to cars. Auntie squeezed the horn to warn them we were coming.'

'The seats were made of shiny leather.'

'We put up the roof when it rained.'

'There was no boot for luggage, so we strapped it on the back.'

Tool chest

Spare tyre

'We stepped on to a running board to get in, because the car was so high.'

'There were hardly any garages. We bought petrol at a hardware shop and carried a spare can on the running board.'

SHELL MOTOR SPIRIT

'The windscreen helped to protect the driver, but we were blown about in the back seats.'

'The headlights were so dim, we always came home before dark. Auntie never went out at night.'

V 2948

Starting handle

'Mudguards stopped dirt from splashing up.'

2000   1975   1950

Great-granny told me
people could get dirty and cold
driving in an open car.

The roads were very bad —
dusty in dry weather
and muddy in wet weather.
Most people wore driving clothes.

Dustcoat

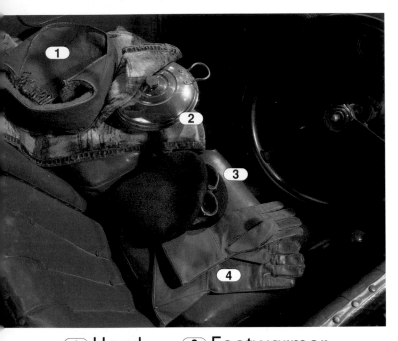

① Hood   ② Footwarmer
③ Goggles   ④ Gauntlets

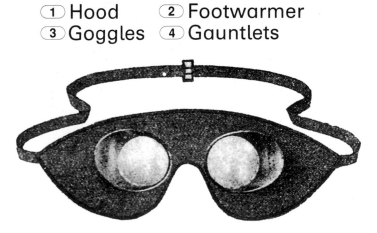

Goggles   Hood

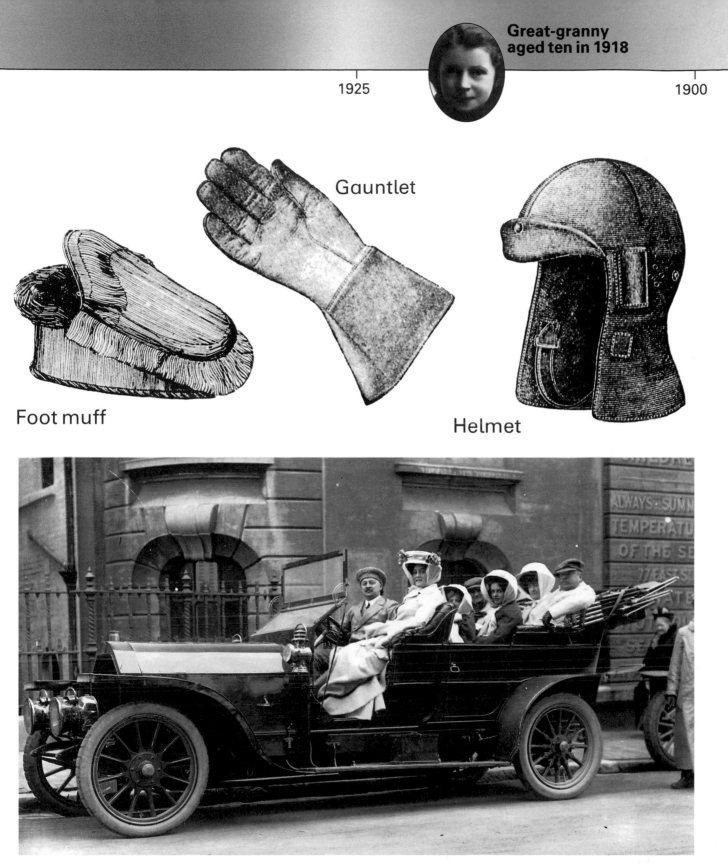

Gauntlet

Foot muff

Helmet

In cold weather, people wrapped up in thick clothes and put a rug over their knees.

Timeline

1884-1909	1910-1919	1920-1929	1930-1939

1884-1885 The motor car was invented by Karl Benz.

1896 A 12 mph (19 km/h) speed limit was set.

1897 The RAC (Royal Automobile Club) was formed.

1903 A 20 mph (32 km/h) speed limit was set.

1903 The driving licence was introduced.

1905 The AA (Automobile Association) was formed.

1908 The first Model-T Ford car was built.

1911 Electric lights and starters began to appear on new cars.

1912 The Morris Oxford car was launched.

1914 The Model-T van was built. Traders started to use horse-drawn carts, rather than vans, for local journeys.

1914 The first car assembly line was built by Ford in the United States of America.

1919 The Ministry of Transport was established.

1922 The Austin Seven car started to be built.

1926 Safety glass windows started to be used in cars.

1927 White lines were used for the first time to divide the road.

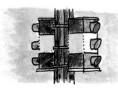

1928 The first traffic lights appeared, in Wolverhampton.

By the end of the twenties, petrol stations had become a more common sight.

In the thirties, the first by-passes were built, along with the first roundabouts.

1934 The first pedestrian crossings with Belisha beacons were introduced.

1934 The driving test was introduced

1935 The Highway Code became law.

1935 A 30 mph (48 km/h) speed limit was established in built-up areas.

1935 The Ford Popular car started to be built. It cost £100.

1939 The Second World War began. Petrol rationing started.

1940-1959	1960-1969	1970-1979	1980-1990s
During the War, car manufacture came to a halt. **1945** A basic petrol ration was allowed again for private cars. **1950** Wartime petrol rationing ended. **1958** The first motorway opened. **1958** Parking meters were introduced. **1959** The Morris Mini was launched.	**1960** The MoT test for roadworthiness was introduced. **1961** Already one million Morris Mini cars had been sold. **1963** From this time, there was a move towards more pedestrianised streets. **1965** A 70 mph (112 km/h) speed limit was established on motorways. **1967** Breathalyser tests to clamp down on drink-drive were introduced. **1969** The Ford Capri was launched. **1969** Pelican pedestrian crossings were introduced.	An energy crisis loomed so there were long queues for petrol and rising petrol prices. **1971** A Lunar Roving Vehicle was used by the first men on the moon. **1972** Spaghetti Junction opened in Birmingham. **1977** British Leyland car production was halted by a massive strike amongst its workers.	The Japanese produced more cars than the United States of America, for the first time. **1983** Front seat belts had to be worn by law. **1983** Wheel clamping started. **1986** The M25 ring road around London was completed. **1986** Unleaded petrol was introduced. **1991** By law, safety belts had to be worn in the rear seat of cars.

Things to do

Look at these four cars.
Which is the oldest? Which is the newest?
What things about them are different?
What is still the same?

What is your favourite car?
Find out about its history.
Make a scrapbook about it.

Ford production line 1914

Index

Photographs: courtesy of The Automobile Association 28; BMIHT/Rover Group cover (br), 7(b); courtesy of the Co-operative Society 13(b); Mary Evans Picture Library cover (main picture), 26(br); Chris Fairclough Colour Library title page(b), 4(c), 5(b); courtesy of the Ford Motor Company Ltd 31(all); Francis Frith Collection 20-21; courtesy of the Harlow Study and Visitors Centre 10(b); Hulton Picture Company 13(c), 15(t), 19, 27(b); Imperial War Museum 18(tr), 18(b); Peter Millard 12(b), 13(t), 17(b), 23(br); courtesy of National Car Parks Ltd 4(b); National Motor Museum, Beaulieu 6(t), 8(t), 8(c), 9(cr), 9(cl), 9(b), 16(b), 23(bl), 24-25, 26(tl), 26(bc), 30(t), 30(cl), 30(b); Popperfoto 16(cl); courtesy of Nic Portway 22(tl), 26(tr), 26(bl), 27(tl), 27(tc), 27(tr); Quadrant Picture Library cover (tl), endpapers, title page (t), 8(b), 9(tl), 11(t), 23(t); Rex Features 10(tr), 11(b); courtesy of The Royal Automobile Club 28; reproduced by kind permission of Shell U.K. Ltd 15(c), 15(b); courtesy of Anthea Shovelton cover (tr); courtesy of Tesco Creative Services 5(t); Topham 14(t), 14(b), 17(t); courtesy of Vauxhall Motors Ltd 4(t), 30(cr); Zefa cover (br).